SHEARSMAN
125 & 126

WINTER 2020 / 2021

EDITOR
TONY FRAZER

Shearsman magazine is published in the United Kingdom by
Shearsman Books Ltd
P.O. Box 4239
Swindon   SN3 9FL

Registered office: 30-31 St James Place, Mangotsfield, Bristol BS16 9JB
(this address not for correspondence)

www. shearsman.com

ISBN 978-1-84861-737-7
ISSN 0260-8049

Subscriptions and single copies

Current subscriptions – covering two double-issues, each around 100 pages in length – cost £17 for delivery to U.K. addresses, £20 for the rest of Europe (including the Republic of Ireland), and £22 for the rest of the world. Longer subscriptions may be had for a pro-rata higher payment. Purchasers in North America will find that buying single copies from online retailers in the U.S.A. or Canada will be cheaper than subscribing, especially since the drastic price-rises for mail to the U.S.A. in mid-2020. This is because copies of the magazine are printed in the U.S.A. to meet orders from online retailers there, and thus avoid the transatlantic mail.

Back issues from nº 63 onwards (uniform with this issue) cost £9.95 / $17 through retail outlets. Single copies can be ordered for £9.95 direct from the press, post-free within the U.K., through the Shearsman Books online store, or from bookshops. Issues of the previous pamphlet-style version of the magazine, from nº 1 to nº 62, may be had for £3 each, direct from the press, where copies are still available, but contact us for a quote for a full, or partial, run. The single-copy retail price as of 2020 is £9.95.

Submissions

Shearsman operates a submissions-window system, whereby submissions may only be made during the months of March and September, when selections are made for the October and April issues, respectively. Submissions may be sent by mail or email, but email attachments are only accepted in PDF form. We aim to respond within 3 months of the window's closure, i.e. all who submit *should* hear by the end of June or December, although we have sometimes taken a little longer.

This issue has been set in Arno with titling in Argumentum. The flyleaf is set in Trend Sans.

Contents

Jill Jones

Undo Everything

I resurrect the dead for a second when I close my eyes
remembering the spring and the sea.
I look at each plant for belief or breath.

Sorrow isn't something I'd name.

Knots are possibilities. I weave them
out of themselves, tenderly, curiously, like a charm.
There are cold things I can't brush away.

How everything has shifted.

Sky's beautiful dry shadows fall on my pages
through the familiar spectrum.
I remember the taste of water.

'I will let loose my longing.'

Maybe there's also that weird glimmer
of hope or fantasy that now itches along
with the lies I told.

Cup water and spill it, undo everything.

I am alone yet among a great crowd, ravens
gather in the old dead tree, there are minutes
that remember me when I still don't know myself.

Everything hurts, so, maybe that's the case.

I'm leaning into the darkness yet again.
I have boxes of medicine for everything. I think about
dreams of mutiny and burn the poems.

Even the yellow door is sighing.

When rain doesn't come, it's still a sound
in the earth. In the lateness every hour retreats.
In these shiftings   something unexpected

which isn't sorrow.

The Moon, Antares, and the Dead As Well

'The problem of time is like the darkness of the sky' —John Berger

We don't see our faces in the stars, tonight, or any night.
They're older than faces.
What do we do with the problem of time? I wonder what rivers do.
Or estuaries, atoms, clouds, constellations, in their time.
All those traces as threads, so even the absent are present.
The dead as well.
As though there's a perimeter, an edge to the realm-that's-not-us.

Look, there's the past, the crescent moon! And above it Venus
then Jupiter, and further up the sky, Antares in Scorpius.
The moon's light takes just over a second to reach our faces.
That light from Antares left itself just before the birth of Galileo.
Always a past touches us, as this hot January forgets us.
To imagine Galileo on such a night, as if he might walk here still
through us. Looking for ancient heat above this heat.

This pulse of a big, old story is far from our traffic and trees
our ground's levels and hollows. We don't hear it.
We can only think and feel into this time, our time
that remembers the living and 'all-that-the-living-are-not'.
But the dead aren't us.
Nor are they stars, despite all the names up there.
Someone left a beer bottle next to the street tree.

I hear voices in a yard nearby.
Who's speaking at this hour, charging the night?
Maybe in the dark, things are more tolerable.
Maybe in the dark you're not yet born.
Tonight's cold thin moonlight falls onto their faces.
Hear them laughing, not loudly.
Like a conspiracy. Of being with. Maybe together, outside.

Close your eyes and keep them open.
Maybe turned upwards into the past,
towards each other now.
The past as now to come.
Where we are also in past light
coming light.

[The two phrases in quotes are from John Berger, *and our faces, my heart, brief as photos.*]

How To Write (or How Not To)

I don't know how to   *Think of a sentence.*
I don't know how   *Visibly comforting.*

I don't know how to   *Close it.*
I don't know how   *Let's be all well.*

I try some more   *A veritable hope.*
Can I still do this   *Hours follow.*

It is hard when   *Let her press.*
The night follows me   *It makes theirs a present.*

The dumbness strikes like   *Take nothing.*

———

Think of a sentence like a plan that is not going well
Visibly comforting and so much more fun

Close it up as a power grab and then go into all the noise
Let's be all well enough for the rest

A veritable hope is the worst thing
Hours follow me back to my computer and I'll tell you what you want

Let her press it out of the room
It makes theirs a present for the people who need it

Take nothing for granted that is not too late
Think of a sentence of death and the now

———

I don't know how to think of a sepulchre.
I don't know how to close it.

Can I still do this, when housebreakers follow?
The dumbness stripteases like a nuance.

[The words in italics, and as repeated further into the poem, were selected at random from Gertrude Stein's book, *How To Write*. The text in the second part of the poem was produced using predictive text on a smartphone. The text in the third part was, in part, produced by an N+7 procedure.]

Jodie Dalgleish

The Birdman
(on hearing the dream of Graciela Iturbide)

I saw a man with a plough, as he moved
the earth
birds were released, over his head, through
his hands
that he raised to them—
birds everywhere, as if he were the birds
because he
went to the field to sow seed; of course,
not any ordinary
seed, and this was also the surprise!

The seed
was the food of all the people around
who stopped
to watch the birds, and the food of all the
children
who waited for them
in their homes, who knew already how to
eat
the air
like song rising from the hot oblivion
of clods
that packed themselves into their fingers
they held against
their throats opened to the tuber of their
lungs.

The seed that had already been planted,
maybe even
in the old times
of the children who leapt from home to
home,

9

breaking a toehold,
into the green sky's mantle as it fell to the
ground, where their fists turned over the soil
and birds
were breathed
by them into the finest particles of the dirt,
in which
this man
would make his furrows from the sprout of
all the
alveoli of all
the people. And he said, 'In my Land.
I shall plant birds.'

Catalogue

(i)   Waking to the birds...

(ii)   The new seal we put on the Bialetti coffee pot.

(iii)   In five minutes, list fifty things you last encountered and loved.
         For example, your list might include: 'holding out my hand to
         that fretful dog, who came and then stayed for a scratch';'the
         long puffs of breeze in my room's white gauze curtain'; 'the wild
         cherries we gathered in Julieta's backyard and put into jars.'
         Remember, there are no right or wrong things to include in
         your list. Keep your fingers moving.

(iv)   The sounds of the viticulturalists ramping up their tractors in
         the street.

(v)   The bed by the window (and the bed as the desk).

(vi)   Open questions are better.

(vii)   The flea market jug I found with the potter's mark AIML KR,
         decorated with light blue and green slips that run downwards
         and (by upending the jug) a dark blue one that runs into them
         (as if upwards) to trace them, like a retreating wave.

(viii)   Breaking the wrong thing.

(ix)   The music, in progress, on the stand of the piano.

(x)   The scan of the verse my dad taught me:'One dark day, in the middle of the night/Two dead men got up to fight/Back-to-back they faced each other/Drew their swords and shot each other.'

(xi)   The plexsitives (expletives) I always see in billboards.

(xii)   The definition I discovered in an old Webster's Dictionary of a 'Cipher Clerk: someone who routinely encrypts and decrypts messages.'

(xiii)   The quick tic-tac-tic of a skateboard down the street.

(xiv)   What (un)known kinds of (un)writable texts?

(xv)   Bare feet on baked concrete, no stones.

(xvi)   Singing to my girlfriend for her birthday.

(xvii)   Anne Mette Hjortshøj tells me that if you overload a kiln with wood, the fire takes the oxygen from the clay to colour it chestnut/reddish brown and sometimes pearl.

(xviii) Following a common blue around, *Polyommatus icarus*: its fringe white, not brindled, and its ventral forewing cell's discoidal spot.

(xix)   Today is actually a blue sky day.

(xx)   Scraps on scraps of paper.

(xxi)   The line inside the curve of my husband's hip.

(xxii)   Walking to the birds, just as the season changed.

(xxiii) If we could rehabilitate the bird to the poem.

(xxiv)   Counting my steps on the stairs.

(xxv)   Time is always a problem:When was that? For how long?

(xxvi)   Today is actually no longer possible.

(xxvii) Keeping the window open.

(xxviii) I wish I could offer up my tongue.

(xxix)   'Lockdown';'Quarantine';'Auto-isolation.' 'Fourteen days.'

Learning to Walk

Your boots press their downwards force into the dirt,
and its deep forest litter. I see their compression of it;
how a heel strikes the distinct trace of your weight, in humus,
and how it rebounds, as if decomposing upwards, our long
hard pressed relations coming back on up, to the arch
as the heft of the body moves itself, onto its toes,
from the great toe, to the second, to the third, and so on:
the body's lift, to the 'toe-off,' and the load of the stance
phase of the gait to be perambulated over ground. How the
valley has loft itself into the strata of schistose rock—time
in foliated, metamorphic rock, up-ended into its mineral
sheaths, sheared along our escarpment: the grand cuts
of orange sericite, green ottrelite, and the sandstone that
has been veined in quartzite, coming up tight and tipped
to the course of our feet. How the heel lifts and is swung
by the foot, in a pendulum, from the hip, to the plant
of the reciprocal leg's pendular pivot; it's like pole-vaulting
off one reiterative stake to the next while the rolling torque
of each hip couples the fall of an arc with the rise of an arc:
how our centre is carried undulately in the constantly, re-
directional, work of our 'step-to-step transitions.' How the
lungs fill to the signals of the receptors in our blood, telling us
how deeply we need to breathe with effort, in the swell
of the belly: sensors at the arterial bifurcation of the throat,
and on the heart's aortic arch, rounding our abdomens out
to the thoracic cavity's influx of air. Where there's a view
from the top of our rock-range spur, over the hook
of the river, its meander that rings it, always, into the setting
of its alluvial settling: our hands out, over the rail,
evidencing, the way all the ridges arrow their way into that
boucle and its almost-island of stone-housed tracts of land.
Stood on the details of its surrounding steeps, it's the 'light touch
contact' of the index finger that will take us back down,
trailing through bracken, and heather: that 'shear force' at the
slightest tip of the 'tactile stimulations of the hand'—that's enough
to maintain 'postural control,' to keep the body's 'equilibrate sway'

in play. To say, how the perennial of bracken succeeds the first forest
ferns and how the perennial of heather (perhaps) branched
from the seeded ones and flowered the first woodlands from which
angiosperms then bloomed: how the fern's helical blades (leafed 'fronds')
have unrolled, and are tri-pinnate—that fractalisation
from rachis (stem) to pinna, pinna to pinnule, pinnule to pinnulet;
their sori that delineate the edge of the smallest 'leaf,' like sutures
of lace; their nectaries that secrete sugars at the base of each branch
of the stem. How heather buds apically too, on branches of leading long
shoots that branch into short shoots, and leading long shoots that branch
into short shoots and leading long shoots: the radial
flower on the hemispherical shrub—that inflorescence of sequential
whorls, of green bracts to dark-stained, mauve calyx, to the pink
petalled corolla and its two stamen-whorls. Its corollate nectary
tucked between pistil's base and anthers' filaments, the undermost
star of the flower. How the apical buds lie dormant below the
(end-of-season) short shoots, and bloom first, if they have
survived, to be followed by the previous years' long-shoot buds,
as they are found alive on the plant; progressing downwards.
When along the 'Long Rock' of the waymarked rim, at 7 AM
in the morning, the sun will hit our escarpment
and burst it into the valley's quartz; flash of the crystalline
éclat of its rock crystal, vitreous lustre tossed out slab-like, light
salvo, under our feet.

Jaya Savige

The Nothing

A hole would be something (Rockbiter)

i.

Compared to The Nothing that is nowhere
yet engulfs all Fantasia
in the *NeverEnding Story*, all other celluloid villains
a child encounters seem vanilla:

none of Scar, the Queen of Hearts, Cruella de Vil,
Sid Philips, Voldemort, Vader or Jabba
come close to its sublime incomprehensibility
(perhaps excepting No-Face and Miyazaki's Yubaba).

Years on, you recognised the chasm
in your introductory class on French Existentialism.
Then you saw it everywhere: in Villon and Nin;
Boundary Street; an episode of *Friends*; a windchime;

and later still, in the car park of a crematorium,
say, or a clinical waste disposal bin.

ii. (Falcor)
Thanks to Bastion, I had a decent grip on nihilism
in good time for my first orgasm.

He knew the void, the gist of entropy.

Remember when the ancient turtle sneezed,
and Atreyu blew in the swamp like a windsock,
only to learn that the oracle in the sky
he needed to get to was a squillion miles away?

Then, when quicksand took the white horse Artax:

the off-white blur in the clouds:
just the sweet rope he
needed: Falcor, the plush luckdragon, who came to impress
a generation (and who, to stop The Nothing, Bastion and
all of us squeezed
as we rose, like freshly minted gods
on our way to name the Empress.)

A Nice Derangement of Epitaphs

'This is BBC
World Service. Violin clashes outside the Chinese embassy...'
Mishearings are harmless; they do not embarrass
anyone, and often give you laughing spasms.

The comedic potential of malapropisms
was unlocked by Sheridan
and perfected by *Back to the Future*'s Biff Tannen
(declaring to Marty's mum: 'I'm your Density... Destiny!').

A typo, however, can do your head in. Typos are serious.

Think of the editor's stony face
when neither spellcheck nor the subs notice
the cub reporter on the landmark IVF case
mangling the judge's ruling that *he could not condom*

such behaviour; or the paroxysm of rage, as the front page
goes out (too soon?) screaming of an *Untied Kingdom*.

Whatever the question, the cordless

leaf blower is his answer most Sundays. Ergonomic, instant start, cruise
control—it's optimal for managing a plot.
      It works a dream
      for purging light
debris, but comes into its own in turbo mode, with soggy cuttings, sods
and rotting limes. He works in bursts, strafing the drive with semiautomatic
jets, and in the rests day's quietude pathetically returns

like a wallaby cradled in a fire blanket. He is there still, wearing only the
pink briefs of dusk, herding into a nice pile the last outstanding invoice.
With one more pass he could well whisk
      the tantalising clod
      of muck that ruins
everything. Manoeuvring the nozzle, he swells the tattered shade cloth like a
god, and sails west beyond all monologue.

Julie Maclean

In flagrante delicto   *i.m. Mirka Mora*

As we witnessed her worldly goods
craned to the back of a truck

we lost count of big-eyed babushkas, earth-bound cushions,
empty frames waiting for a thought.

She was poised under the eaves of heaven
brushing swallows from her hair

chain-smoking Gitanes
a bottle of St Emilion at her winged feet
as Japanese masks of a couple

/he with a cracked cheek
from being dropped in '87/

made their chalk-faced way
to the mountain.

Ravines and rift valleys
formed by boxes of books

gave off the smell of old forests,
dry rivers, death in the Gulag,

death on the land, dead ideas
like truth and adjectives.

And the tribal rug she'd rolled on
over centuries making babies.

We can see it teetering on the summit
in the descending light
stained by blood and love.

Biting the Apple of Barnbougle

On the way to the Lost Farm
a gibbous moon boomerangs off cars
across the Bay of Fires
setting it alight at 3am

The strait is shallow   It's possible to fathom
the migration of souls and thylacines—
something stirs it up out of the Heads—
                a virgin glacier Mawson way
                running from the thing
                that wants to penetrate it

        I am searching for spirits of young black steer
        dissolving in dunes
        foraging in drifts of white middens
        when bumblebees the size of fairy wrens
        swarm around my radiator looking for a piece
        of real estate or dusting of errant pollen

Whop Whop   Looking up a chopper
flies a golf buggy over hand-planted marram
holding the north in place

        At Paper Beach   lagoon and grove
        so Game of Thrones
        I expect Jon Snow to row up in a Viking longship
        and start chipping oysters off the conglomerates
        already gaping open   forced by a tern
or grey gull with no pity

Somebody's been there
Somebody's always been there in places
you think pristine or impossible

Bitumen stamped with stains in that special
Australian way
Pademelons in varying stages of rot
a devil or two   spotted quolls squeezed flat

All the while smoke blossoms from timber
stacked like the dead along the Tamar

In the Blood

Platelets mutate in a petri dish
margins squeezed out of shape by fever

I need them to be perfectly formed cumuli
reincarnated by oils, prayers and better friends

but they refuse to cooperate
Everyone needs more

than well behaved protein   a simple prognosis
More than the life of a blue veined royal—

the colour purple denoting *Special*
Mitochondria have a mind of their own

Rogue molecules can lay you flat
They do not discriminate

Without simple faith in the clock of the sun
a ticking bomb

takes root at your feet
Cells mutate   in all weather

Makyla Curtis

water lines

the water lifts us and shudders
sediment drenched, there is a familiar swallow
a reticence

my throat looks west and south
like two clouds
it marks the move from point A to point B

the oar reaches in and
pushes at our debris, climbs the chanting
of our impositions

each stroke of the water
leads us further through a network
rivers in lines meandering across pages

there is a way here. it is possibly at a depth
that I cannot draw

a tongue tears home reaching for subduction
over and under the sands shudder in speech

at the last crossing was a 2b line
next, the page will end
and my run will cease

this trench so deep I cannot fathom it
thundering black songs down below I cannot
feel them in my throat

I cannot stay here, though I never arrived
at this cleft in the earth, all blue and
sea green

my voice visits, reaching with speech from the cliff
I try to plant my voice here
but the waters wash and wash

Groundwork

we are in light,
a filtered series of dyes   contours of the land
outside the language of colour
I cannot describe this place

chew on the flesh of earth,
aruhe, the root of the bracken

we are in light,
an arrant line across the ink   revisit our fables
we are in the root fibre
of connections   of kin

chew on the flesh of the earth
dried, steeped and roasted

we are in light,
the opening of the sun
among the filmy ferns
and their distance between.

Homecoming

there are only marginalia to the fronds
a record of the archive
        indelible and delicious
there are many homes for our stories in the conjunction points
compound leaves as in compound words

the silver fern arcs over us fragmentary
we arrived inside a fern coil   imaginary   from the earth
        like a home already
               coming home

yet the fern in which we bud is oceans apart
and home is only only
home is
               oceans apart

in the side notes   where the margins
will widen into the main text
the fronds, the other stories, the other homes

but perhaps there will be columns
for the hyphenated.

Helen Tookey

swimming again (Yvonne)

among inverted papayas
a reflected small sun
then Yvonne was swimming again

series of small spouting fountains
fresh mountain water
from the cracked broken hose

hovering over the parapet
hullo, good morning
the object shaped like a dead man

as with a stale thudding of drums
the silence between them
Yvonne   God

finding himself with a dead match
mirroring the sky   aping it
water still trickling into the pool

almost full   still filling
a little turquoise set in the garden
blown fragments of memories

he imagined he still heard the music
immediately below them
the howling sea

for a moment   not holding hands
without speaking   just meeting
then Yvonne was swimming again

Text collaged from Malcolm Lowry, *Under the Volcano*, chapter 3

Citadel

compare the citadel
the citadel and the far edge of the lake
the entire silhouette of the citadel in the water

think of the grays in the citadel
the mortar of the citadel's outer wall
or even the chimney on top of the citadel

the citadel, the walls, the meadow, the cattle
the piling and interlocking of the citadel
the electric calm of the citadel

what happens to the right edge of the citadel
along the center-right of the citadel's second terrace
below the wandering line of the citadel's wall

on the path by the meadow, in the citadel windows
where the sun hits the terrace wall of the citadel
on top of the bank below the citadel

looking out from windows well up in the citadel
there is a last white citadel up there
smoke from a fire way off behind the citadel

Text collaged from T.J. Clark, *The Sight of Death: An Experiment in Art Writing*

New Brighton

This place again – odd angle
where land meets water, river

turns sea. Tide going out fast,
riffling backwards

over ridged brown sand.
Straight out to sea, wind turbines

pecking at the water
like tall white wading birds.

Guarding the river, the shut fort,
built for an invasion

that never happened. Sandstone hull
sunk in the sand, superstructure

twisted, tilting – radar antennae
still turning, still listening

though to what signals, and who
could be there to receive, decipher –

Fifty yards further out,
the lighthouse, still elegant,

white paint only a little
rust-stained, low down

where the iron ladder clings
to the side, climbs up

to the recessed doorway's
dark slot. Thirty lamps,

three fog bells, stripped out
years ago – now pigeons, nesting

in the roof-beams, dive and flutter
the lantern-room, shadow-flicker

behind the glass, as though trying
to catch our attention

– look
at what's no longer here, are you sure

you won't be glad of them, those lamps
and bells, when your satellites

have all blinked out, when your radio's
full of empty air –

Track

[first day]

We walked out in the morning, the four of us. By agreement we walked without speaking, followed the track past the wheatfields down to the canal. Sun behind a shirr of cloud. Everything warm and moving. The tiny brown sparrows dancing in pairs over the wheat, seeming to sit and ride on the surface of it, flushing up in mild alarm as we passed. The wheat an almost-solid surface, the long spikes on each ear forming a kind of frothy blanket that rustled in the wind, the tiny birds playing and resting on this. How we by contrast often seem too large, out of scale with the world around us. How might we shrink ourselves down?

[second day]

The sun still low but already fierce, the thin cloud burned away early, and the warm wind already strong. We walked with the wheatfield to our left; to our right, the long rows of sunflower plants. The oil we need to cook our food, to keep our machines running. On this day we saw no animals. But I had heard them in the night, skittering overhead, and they found their way into my dream – animals kept from earlier times, in long rows of cages, ready to be let out again when the conditions were suitable. Only somehow they had got out already, everything was in complete confusion, no one knowing what to do.

[third day]

This day on the track things seemed different. Scent of water, clods of earth on the road where some vehicle had passed earlier – leaving its trail, like a kind of animal. Four of us as before, but this time I was walking ahead. Disconcerting, knowing the others were following me but not being able to see them. I could hear their presence in small sounds – their footsteps on the road, the clinking of a metal water bottle. As we got nearer to the bridge I began to feel the not-seeing as a kind of pressure, I began to want to turn round and look. But I felt I was under an interdiction, that looking round was not permitted, would result in some kind of catastrophe.

[fourth day]

I walked alone down the track to the canal. The question being asked was that of heat. The wind had risen again overnight, hot and dry. The wheat hissing, as though in disapproval, and from overhead a strange humming sound, a kind of low-pitched wordless singing – the sound of the wind in the telegraph wires. By the canal, below the lock, I sat in the long grass, in the shade of the trees. A butterfly landed on my arm and stayed there for quite a while, walking in tiny circles, its wings folded: pale brown and yellowish, with a single small black spot on each wing. I could just feel its tiny movements against my skin.

On the way back along the track, a black glint – I thought at first a piece of black glass, but was puzzled by its roundness, a tiny black glass ball. Looking more closely I saw there were others, bubbles forming in the patches of tar on the road surface, perfect spheres of near-liquid black, and at the centre of each, a reddish-gold gleam, garnet-like – the surface of the track beginning to melt, turning back to liquid oil.

Diane Mulholland

The Sea Is Both Green and Blue

Day one
In the centre of the bottle a framework of ribs has appeared, like the curl of an upturned leaf.

Later that day
The frame is wrapped with thin, overlapping planks. Watertight, although there's no water in the bottle. And now the deck paints itself in, back and forth around the hatches, narrow at the bow.

Day two
The masts rise. Ropes uncoil at their ends like the tips of ferns and in less than a day the sails have budded along the cross beams. So tightly packed to begin with, but warming and blooming as I watch. I do watch, and try not to disturb anything.

Day three
The sails lift and settle, although there's no wind in the bottle. They're not white, they are no colour at all, and the sun leaps at their edges. Every detail of the ship is tiny and complete and I can't help admiring it just as a new father can't help counting the fingernails on a baby. It darkens and thickens and grows stronger.

Day five
It's growing into the bottle. Out of the bottle. As the masts reach the curved sky they fold into themselves and the sails pleat in layers. Starboard and port press against the walls like a large bottom in a small chair. The figurehead has grown two twig-like antennae and she has almost reached the cork with her little carved nose.

Day eight
I come down early but it's too late. The bottle is broken and the ship is gone. I get a torch and search the corners of the ceiling and behind the wardrobe. Nothing.

I take the pieces of the bottle and break them smaller, then dissolve them in milk and strain them through muslin. Carded, they are as light as the foaming tops of waves. I get out my spindle and start to spin.

Day thirteen
The thread is finished and I tie it in a skein and dip it in indigo. When I take it out it is green and then blue, or both green and blue at the same time. I fold the skein and lay it in the base of a new bottle. The sea is both green and blue and the sun leaps at its edges. I place the cork in the bottle, then rest my elbows on the table and watch.

Peach Rush

There's a rhythm to the orchard harvest,
pick and sort, store neatly. It's a dance
generations have practised since the farm was young.

But one tree won't play our game.
These peaches won't be hoarded, can't be kept.
They seem to mock our prudent plans, 'Today,' they say,

'or never.' And so we try, as they ripen in a rush
and thud, swollen on the grass. We tire of peach
and start to give them all away, and still they swell

and fall. We haven't learnt to celebrate abundance
and feel sorry when the wasps have them in the end.
They feast like pigs along the sweet skin cracks.

Judith Willson

The Parrot-Keeper's Guide,
by an Experienced Dealer

That it is necessary to slit a parrot's tongue to enable it to talk
is fallacious. Caress the bird. Indulge it with sponge cake fancies,
bean flowers and strawberries in season,
to produce the desired effect.

A Ring-necked Parakeet requires a patient tutor.
If not taken in hand very young it will learn nothing,
content to pass through life lacking accomplishments,
like many an idle girl.

The African Parrot receives the lessons of its teacher
with docility and grace. Apropos of the female Love Bird:
a more surly, ill-tempered little glutton never existed.
She rips out her husband's feathers.

The vivacity of Bengal Parakeets is charming when they perform
their little exercises, their perfect *As-tu déjeuné, Cocotie*?
But they will too often persist in their own speech –
a disagreeable, incessant screeching.

The female Groffins Cockatoo is demure but dull.
I have kept one that never mastered more than two words:
Well and *Martha* repeated in a low timid voice.
The latter was her own name.

Eggs of the Paradise Parrot are white. Turn one in your hand.
So perfect in itself – like a full moon that does nothing
but widen the icy distances over our rooftops.
The shell has a faint lustre, as of marble.

Bradwell power station (decommissioned)

no visible entrance or exit
slab and cube swept by aluminium light

silver / grey / citrine at dusk
each day's parabola as it falls

leaves its soft chaff shadow traces
in flow across a white screen

[Rauschenberg: I called them clocks]

sealed in safestore time burns away
to a pinprick an eyelet into dark

where someone driving through the night
sees for an instant a running creature

drawn out of air caught in flight
for an instant backlit by radiance

West India Dock

a Provident Legislature
the Corporate Body
Complete SECURITY

STABILITY, INCREASE AND ORNAMENT

THE RIGHT HONOURABLE
THE RIGHT HONOURABLE
under the favour of GOD

ILLUSTRIOUS

rums   mahoganys   dye-woods
sugar warehouses   crystallising sugar*   its lustre

*free-grown in casks
slave-grown in boxes   distinct

O barley-sugar temples   O dainties

riches of the universe poured at her proud feet

100,000 tons at the Import Dock
4 men winching each crane
walls 20 foot high   iron gates   a guardhouse
Weighers & Searchers
counting houses mounted on wheels

CONTRIVANCES & BONDS

Mr Hibbert, plantation owner
West India merchant upwards of forty years:
the plunderer is very ingenious

Maria Stasiak

Archivist

It was dusk but the sky
shone yellow
like a backwards dawn.

The crows were black on grey and
blinking, serious,
watching the first step.

And the houses turned away
as I went past.
The city shied away from me.

Understand that I was not
assassin.
I was archivist.

I came to trace your story
bring back pieces
for the tapestry, the shroud.

Behind the staggered junctions
and the grieving
streets I looked for you.

We lay inside that tiny
terraced house beside the by-pass
laughing across the dark

bound in blood and
flashing into life with lorry-lights
across the roundabout

matches striking out
discarded from your fingers
into the tin dish.

You'd have got it, this dislocated
space, this passage through
a night-time, anchored and adrift.

Streaked across the buildings
and my face
the rain blew in like judgement.

Lightning lifted up the sky
and let it drop.
I journeyed solitary, surrendered.

Far behind my back
the daylight gathers, vastly over-
whelms this restless night.

I'm left against a doorway
wrapped in grey
withdrawing into stillness.

We're diffusing, you and I,
like bruises lifting, lightening
into pale thin sky.

Disordered

After the edges of the world
snapped shut, and we found out
there was no *out there*
any more, nowhere to hunt
redemption or success,
we sold our neurochemistry
in cool creative ways,
and it was bad for us and we
knew it but had no strange clue
how to do otherwise,
and having taken the mammal's route,
the busy worried churning up
of soil, the fretful sore
outrunning of desire,
and rejected the reptile's
silent keeping of position
as the bad times pass,
we came out fighting,
crowded with anger and reckless
with cheap charm,
because it always was
an odd request, to see *other*
as *us*, to know the ambitious poverty
of our designs, and we are
not very good at it
not very good at all.

After we gave in to *advantage*
because everything was built on
advantage, and deification of
the way things ought to be
solidified our expectation
that there would always be *more*
always be *better*,

we realised we had no wisdom
none at all, but were only
restless for adventure,
and having confected sentiment
as truth, self-righteousness
as worth, and sought to fill
the far too fat expansion of our minds
with *busyness,*
we felt the blood-trail run
disordered in our arteries,
tangle through the black exhaust
adrenaline that's rushing in
the roadway, pausing time
and we were
not very good at looking out for ourselves
not very good at all.

After we fucked up
and refused to make apology
because the mockery was
unendurable and so was being wrong,
and bad repute began to seem
a novel and ingenious idea,
it began to dawn on us that we had no
faint notion how to play
any of it, and having feasted on
suspicion, plot, the tiny
unappeasable discrepancies
which filled us up completely
filled us up with
richness, comfort, certainty
and rage, and whispered us
against our fellows vigilant in dark,
we realised in the end
the most effective strategy
the best technique

was probably *distraction,*
and we were pleased with ourselves
because *distraction* is an infinite
enjoyable resource, and we are
good at it. Damned good.

After the violence

When we finally found you
six months after
the crime, the violence
you were thrown in woodland
and you were all decayed

taken in the care of those
who knew what to do with you
creatures evolved in expectation
of this mute unrushed
attention to your flesh.

Within the forest floor
they found you first
breaching the skin, the
horror, your body salvaged
in these tiny rapid lives.

It's quiet here, after
what must have been
shouting, screams.
But never think it's lonely
under the trees.

Never think you weren't
attended to, accompanied.

Kate Ashton

for the boy who wept at Fauré's Requiem

i
borage blue sky unclouded as cobalt
eye old stone fenestrate place
star

smitten upturned face glazed gold azure
dazed cherubim swum troubled
jade

of inturned sea caught piteously pray
for me a little birth a lamb low
born

ii
in blood and snow opal apostle
fist of flame names Jack James
Stephen

Latin carved in old black oak aback
white lace framed face
sinless

iii
as love's plainsong a prayer
flown apse altarless bare
as ages stripped

iv
of singing stone echoing holy
Mary muse a requiem
for them a

men another Kyrie eleison a son
a mother seated in the choir
calm beauty

v
beneath reaching roof
of upturned ark steep
stern drop

dream deep drown the boy
is lost at sea head bowed
suddenly she

sees he is weeping averts her gaze
preserves his dignity he
rubs his eyes ten

vi
years eleven maybe I see
he gives me glass he
gives me sliding

river flow sepia sky above
shy upturned glaze of stone
and dispensation

at last he gives me grace to melt
like glass-eyed sky or sealed
sepulchre of salt

vii
become sprung rainbow heart
sung open as the Book
of Life itself

Rubens Red

Something Flemish maybe, weight,
ornate gilt-listed reflection, high
ceiling cornice swagged and bare
pale cluster at the rose

or was it the Grassmarket's open
throat, a-glitter gasp of last repose,
a scintillating perfumed pulse
echo of emptied artery,

no urgency, no force, Grande Place
forgetful of its double tongue,
true iteration of the wooded
edge where once the doe

described her arc indelibly
and night transcribed it into
trembled time as slow
processions of leapt dark, or

perhaps felled stand of onyx
flesh, architrave crowned with
outraged frown, small footfall
in mid-air, clawed cheek,

lost clutch, hot bloodless breast
that mourns itself to stony
death, long loosed locks become
shriek-shroud for bluing son,

too much milky measure hurled
headlong into silken lap where
no cry holds, a stifled slide through
carmine pleat and fold –

and then Kaddish between the thighs
soft intimation of desire, blank
affirmation mirrored in the hall,
slow dawning crimson climb

as step by step in its own time
bright spill made spate sure as all
destiny, something fulfilled,
another fate than mine.

Daragh Breen

Lear with Antlers

Boxed by the white glare of the lift
in the dark realm
of a multi-storey car park basement,
he is stooped as he wrestles with
what began to bramble from his skull
in the wilderness
and as he stumbles forward
the ceiling lights tumble on one by one
as he looks around for someone
that he can articulate to
the emptiness that he had witnessed

like the astronaut who travelled
along the length
of a mountain-side track in Nepal,
lined with school children
who knelt
with lit candles as he passed,
as he had walked
among their ancestors on the moon,
yet had failed to see anybody.

The Lamb of God Enters a
Handball Alley in Connemara

Trailing a clogged-spittle of afterbirth
as if she'd been grazing on plastic bags,
the ewe nudges the wet mess of her lamb
into the shelter of the handball alley,
a triptych of concrete walls,

an Icon stripped of its gold Russian snow,
as a seagull spreads the altar of its wings
and rises,
     while above,
          in the deep dark,
a satellite continues to blink on its orbit,
beyond which the censer of Saturn shimmers
incense,
     and further still,
          the tangled thorn tree of the
Milky Way comes into flower,
          while below,
within the Earth's sight, the tarnished disc
of the Sun slides behind rain clouds,
which will surely now begin to fall.

Mustard Gas

Garlanded with rubber ventilators
the fog of their lung-snouts
echoing in their ears,
newly shod with trench foot
and just one more death away from madness
a sudden owl mistakes all those
staring back from their long open grave
for brethren.

Rosaries of light are born in the years-deep dusk
as below, the earth's surface consumes itself
horses' eyes staring back from
within the mud and the war glue,
Death already occupies
multiples of the strewn Great Coats
yet men still try to struggle into them
for warmth or for company.

Janet Sutherland

Falls from Horses

By the second night in the saddle
I was reeling backwards and forwards
in an odd and ridiculous manner.
So black was the whole horizon,
so dense the forest through which we passed,
that although the Tatar had a white horse
we rode in loneliness all night.

Descending a hill my horse fell hard
in ground so soft I lay unharmed,
the roads quite saddle-girth high in mud,
my ears dinned by the howling of wolves.
In grey dawn my horse fell again
twisting the spur on my right boot
to a scrap of bent wire. Those hours
of watchfulness and mud!

I rode near the brink of precipices
through defiles that closed overhead
deep in trance till a nearby muezzin
called out the earliest prayer.
He called me to wakefulness too,
the dawn light tender on the mountains.
How thankful I am to Him who has thus
been merciful through this long journey!

*From a Letter of Colonel Charles Townley, Queen's Foreign Service Messenger,
riding from Belgrade to Therapia in November 1849*

Belgrade Fortress, 2018

I took no notes, but the photos say we were there,
high up, looking over the Danube,
the Danube and the Sava at the place where they join,
on the 25th of September at 4.32.
It was sunny and bright, each cloud haloed,
everything bleached, the rivers wore bands of silver,
even the small path that slanted down
to the overlook above a busy road
had moon-white paving. By the side of the path
a drystone wall retainer
and at every step, I remember, there were lizards
first splayed and motionless then gone
one after the other, basking in the heat then gone.
It was then you told me, and I don't know why
it seems important to remember this,
how on another day, you'd seen a car lose all control
spinning across both carriageways,
the noise of it, and then

Lucy Hamilton

The Red Jars

For Ms Ying Chen

Each morning the two jars respond to the day's glow
filtering through our roof's red window blinds

How elegant they are| here on the glass table
where they swell| drum-bulbous with a just pride

The low-framed table requires no further adornment
since the jars speak eloquently for themselves

their red bellies pregnant with sound & memory
I remove the black lids| and leaves dry as brown grass

fill them with fresh water| each to a disparate level
and tap out a rhythm with my bamboo chopsticks

I think of the ancient Jingdezhen mountain forests
and the valleys| where 'ten thousand men' stacked kilns

and fired ceremonial drums made of clay & kaolin
dyed in blood & cinnabar| decorated with cowries

Bewitched by tradition| villages danced to the drumbeat
aroused by the yin-yang dynamic of its power & spirit

Bi • Adorning

The Master Craftsman Weaves a Bamboo Vase

Gripping the blade in his right hand and bamboo
in his left| Mr Xu splits the wood lengthways

and lets the two pieces fall onto the pile at his feet
On the wall above| *Ascending the River at Qingming*

evokes ancient scenes I saw from a Fuzhou train
of graves strewn with flowers| This weaving frieze

flows the width of the workshop wall| like the river
where junks once heaved abundant cargos of cane

He softens the strips in water and plaits the supple
threads into a three-metre vessel which lies on its side

Stubble-ends bristle around the lip of its open mouth
mimicking the jutting bean stems in the ideograph

In the old Chinese tradition he will exhibit the vase
at his house| one of a pair to keep his family safe

Now he takes up a black-dyed strand to complete
the face of the First Emperor| interlacing his memory

Feng • Abundance

The Elephant with Three Tusks

When I stroked the life-size green jade elephant
outside the Chalan Temple I hadn't yet seen the bone

ideogram of the animal standing up on its hind legs
long trunk swaying in the air| nor the image

of two hands holding a small object in a gesture
of giving and receiving| Here just north of the 'Cradle

of the Revolution'| I knew that herds of elephants
were once employed for war as well as for transporting

heavy timber| as I knew that local folk had delighted
in dancing the 'elephant dance'| Story goes that only

twenty-five years ago a wealthy businessman dreamt
he saw himself renounce his excess and build this temple

The green jade is from Myanmar and the three tusks
symoblise king and the elephant's special relationship

with Buddha| They say that Siddhārtha Gautama sang
while entering his mother's womb as a white elephant

Yü • Delight

Calligraphy by Sophie Song.

Guy Birchard

Old Mexico

Here we go, see?

Dirt road in country rattletraps drive—
Mine, the Stranger's, must brake
for what's coming through the floorboards.

> Pickup overtakes, loaded with
> campesinos obliged to stop too,
> me being in the way. They don't object...

We all pile out. Gracious, gentle men smile, say,
This is special place
and these Holy Days.

> *Yes. Young girls come*
> *seeking*
> *blessing of the Snakes...*

Music like never before heard, from an instrument so
big it takes two to play, one fretting, one plucking,
fast trance/dance, melodious exotica.

> There goes a bevy of señoritas
> over the crest of a hill.
> Hombres smile, nod.

¡Dog in tall grass has caught a snake! By God,
snakes plural all around underfoot—so leap! me,
aerial footwork a whole while to keep off of 'em!

> No one else is bothered...
> Paisanos, accustomed, want nothing
> of gringo, of vestals.

Trampled into the verdure: big, weathered broadsides—
Yanqui poems *from before the Revolution leftover.*
I can have 'em if I want 'em, nobody minds.

> My truck they have fixed, U-turned
> toward the Main Route. Can I
> ford that creek, bottom of the hill?

Go, pobrecito, there is no problem here.

Of a Bathing Suit (One-Piece) from the Desert
(excerpt)

It may only be nostalgia, this barely discernible, barely intelligible current in the bygone stirring the present.

Intense cold in Saskatchewan. You think you know. You don't know. Into a headwind to boot, all day the gauge showed no temp at all, despite insulating cardboard jammed between grill and rad.

Cavalierly passing semis beyond Great Falls in white-out after white-out.

In the second lucky break (the first, to have managed to come to this Pass, period), bald eagles roosted everywhere in elevated calm between Deer Lodge and Monida

before that *CROSS-*

WIND to wrestle like the Angel down into Idaho Falls, enough to blow Greyhound and transporter off the road.

Three days out, in no end of inclemency, as far south as Utah, heavy, wet, unplowed slush, thick, for the crush of amateur winter drivers commuting between Ogden and Salt Lake City.

What is the word for the solace of a finally mild, moist, blissfully dull January Nevada desert's sweet, false lull?

Delusion?

Penultimately, overnight in Barstow, a plot point-perfect derailment spilling something toxic across the Interstate closed, presciently, our narthex, the Cajon Pass.

Nothing for it but to detour all the way west toward Tehachapi before deking south at State Route 58's wide spot—called "Mojave"

: triggering memory of the white one-piece she bought in the Navajo Nation along I-40 anticipating beaches seven hundred miles to go nigh twenty years before…

Butterflies & Turtle

In-country small-*i* illegally, navigating a hundred-buck Ford Capri, hight *The Brown Bum*—on an important mission: escorting the girl to Hollywood.

Cracked plug wires had given them grief in a squall in Iowa but here we find them in humid, sun-bombed Missouri.

In a backroad hamlet they bought a bunch of baby carrots, a sack of *Guy's Brand Bar-B-Q Potato Chips* and a six-pack of *Miller High Life* to put on ice.

Call the vignette: *Rest Area with Picnic Bench in Shade by Crick*.

He twisted the tops off the carrots and tossed the handful into tall grass. Then, bethinking himself—civic tidiness—went to retrieve it.

The bundle of carrot tops had happened to land pretty much on the nose of a snapping turtle. Snapper reared back on its hinder end, gaped cantaloupe-colored gullet wide enough to make the intended impression—and *hissed* at him. Hissed at him.

Miles along, they found a campground all to themselves beside some *Van Meter* family, Civil War-era graveyard. Under a full moon, no less.

Exiting the cinder block shower next morning, not a soul around, sunlit, stepping into his gotches, his shoulders and damp, bare back were suddenly a drift of Painted Ladies alighting.

Guy fetches the camera a look of small-*c* concern.

Tupa Snyder

Flight to India
To Jake and beginnings

Decades down, I will remember you
looking out of our bedroom window
at gentle horse pastures
silvering in autumn where the patchwork
countryside swells and greets me,
the turns in the roads
familiar when I come home from Uni.
The dark soil is alive
with ancient pottery that comes up
in the plough, this history of homes
burrowed in my heart.

I have watched the films
over and over our evenings of separation,
that my parents used to watch
in the ship crossing over to England.
Were things more certain then,
no gutted past
ripping like a skirt from a startled body?
You search for a comfortable place
to hoist your newfound identity
as you start out
from our broken marriage.

I would rather not know
where you are going;
I want this unhinged moment to become
only a beginning. That's what
my parents lived with
all their lives when there wasn't a home

anymore, the nuances of their arrival
in England
interspersed through my everyday
after they returned to India;

as I am doing now. In the beginning
St. Martin's bells were pealing
as we entered Doddiscombsleigh
the first time;
honeysuckle on the kitchen door
of the Nobody Inn,
our own maddened shadows
twinned amongst the hedgerows
as we took it all in. The beauty.
The stretched desire.

Divorce is giving up
the lap of sounds;
lambs belling for an udder
in the afternoon's quiet
as the jazz notes of lovelessness
strum in the belly
of the aircraft going back
to where I started from.

John Levy

Shopping for Groceries Saturday Morning, 2/22/20

A woman stands
in front of the cucumbers I want
to search among, she's

carefully, contemplatively handling small
green chili pepper after small green chili pepper.
I think she, like me, is nearing the age of 70.

I am loathe, as the saying goes, to ask her
to move for a moment. The little shapely bodies
she picks up and puts down, shiny green, dented, twisted,

gleam. I return three
minutes later and there she is, still inspecting those
lost little lives that a sculptor would be, could

be, should be proud of
if she sculpted them, but she didn't and I believe
the seed had no pride

at any stage of the process. Pride comes
before the fall has no
meaning to a seed, nor to the sun the seed requires

to become a small pepper being handled by an old
pair of eyes. I go some place else a minute, she
doesn't. Standing beside her I quickly find

cucumbers for my daughter's salads, rejecting
one in four unlike this expert's apparent rejection
of nine out of ten peppers. Maybe she's a painter?

Maybe she's in no rush to go home. Maybe
she's composing an ode, silently, without a need
to write it down because her memory

is 10 times better than mine. Maybe
in this floating world
she loves the drift and sadness (uki) of life (yo).

We are both upright and breathing, near
hundreds of mushrooms, cucumbers, peppers,
zucchini, and several thoughts

in our heads depend
only partly on what we see and what
we want to see. We were both children

at about the same time, perhaps both
looked in the mirror in sixth grade wishing
we could know how we'd look as grown-ups.

How disappointed would those sixth graders be
if they stood off to the side, observing us
in our late 60s? Would it even occur to those kids

that we both made it through more than 50 years
of countless ways we could've perished before now?
Would they think, "No, there must be some mistake!"

(Note to John Phillips, 2/28/20)

So I'm going to Google "birds associated with death" and after typing the
first two words the search gives me, first, the final two words. It must be
the most common search beginning with "birds associated" or is Google
reacting to my own past searches? Probably not, since the third most

popular search is "birds associated with christmas" and there is nothing in my search history to suggest that that would be on my mind.

Here we go:

birds associated with death
birds associated with time
birds associated with christmas (lower case, that is per Google, not me)
birds associated with magic
birds associated with fire
birds associated with healing
birds associated with the sun

Wikipedia: "Certain animals such as crows, cats, owls, moths, vultures and bats are associated with death; some because they feed on carrion, others because they are nocturnal."

It is a Friday. Twelve minutes ago it was 11:11 a.m. in Tucson and 8:11 p.m. in Athens, as I was writing an email to Vassilis Zambaras in Greece. Now, twelve minutes later, I'm surrounded by certain animals such as crows, moths, bats, owls, and cats; some because I read the Wikipedia entry. Alright, all of them because I read that entry. Entry into the land of creatures feeding on carrion and/or considered nocturnal. It will never be 11:11 a.m. in Tucson on February 28th, 2020, again. Is stating that fact similar to feeding on carrion?

Tomorrow is leap day. This fact doesn't fit in to anything mentioned above. It leaps over everything mentioned above and stays suspended in the air. It isn't a fact with wings, though, not here. It has two legs. It has been personified. In another paragraph it could be crowified, but it won't be.

Hello dearie. No one said that just now. I'm alone. I'm not sure why I thought of it. How many years has it been since someone called me "dearie"? Probably the women who called me that, in my past, have passed away. Did I think of it because this bit of writing is, as a friend of mine might say, deathsoaked?

John Phillips

Prague   *for Naomi Frears*

The painting was titled *Prague*, the city where the artist spent her honeymoon. In the centre was a white metal bed and the head of a young man. Behind the man's head, the erased image of a tree. Two small, delicate impressions of branches – one at the top of the painting, one on the bottom left. Almost invisible. The ghost of grid-lines over-or-under-lay everything else.

For the artist, the bed was an erotic symbol. Jasna and I thought it the bed in which Gregor Samsa awoke. The man's head even reminded us of Kafka.

The artist said the pencilling of transparent grids was a substitute for her desire to smoke. Sartre wrote whoever smoked imagined each time they lit a cigarette they were destroying the world.

Jasna noticed the man had no lips. She said this deepened his silence. I thought it a silence coiled around a scream.

After we'd hung the painting above the fire, she lay down in her thin dress on the white metal bed, hugged her knees to her stomach and wept.

Windows

My words don't have to be thinking the same thing I am, unless they say what they're thinking to me. If they keep their thoughts to themselves, what they think is invisible. Sometimes the moon is invisible. The distance between my thoughts and the words which express my thoughts might be the same as the distance between the moon and myself. I can't calculate where to begin that thought and my words don't want to. In the sunlight, in the moonlight, distance is different. There are buildings without windows from which to see the moon. Some thoughts are windows.

WHICH HAPPENS

Wittgenstein wrote, "In philosophy the winner of the race is the one who can run the most slowly. Or: the one who gets there last".

I misread this as saying: Or the one who gets there lost.

I prefer that.

Arriving at the destination long desired
only to not know where you are,

or why.

To Hew

chop or cut with an axe,
a pick, some other tool,
carpenters hew logs with an axe,
to hack, hack down, cut down, fell, lop, cleave, to destroy
   the living, cut off parts of the living from the living,
   to make or shape by cutting out a tree fallen, say
   to carve, to fashion, hammer, chisel and sculpt
   steps hewn into rock wall, to conform or adhere to,
   to hew to high ethical standards, at times close to cleave,
   to cling to

from Old English hēawan, of Germanic origin,
related to Dutch houwen, to German hauen

can be used to describe words
hewn from language out of silence

Giles Goodland

Over

His arms back over his head
Sand turns over the narration
roads web over the planet
gulls yawk over like street vendors
hold equal dominion
soar over the red roof-tiles
Brunel's bridge over the Brent
or over single-pole bridges
over 95,000 flights cancelled
shivering over the whole body
adverts plastered all over him
the river turns over small stones
pours its waters over a precipice
this is turned over to the note teller
spirit places a hand over it
clouds are bricked over
click on an arrow to turn over
over the next two turns
wind is driven over the bottle
the moon over the trees
the cock is rubbed over the axe
fixed over gates and doors
over a wide geographic range
pressure over the diaphragm
the transfinite towers over the finite
over a 131-meter beam distance
white silk is drawn over red silk
wind running over barley
rejects rocks over 380 mm
any male over forty years old
survival jacket over the torso harness

the pipes play over the funeral
chieftain of over 1,000 tents
spread over the vast night city
control you have over content
pisses over the pastel of me as a boy
over the full travel of a screw
a wastewater ditch washes over him
the gums close over the areola
cage-cloak over a white mini dress
over baggy boyfriend trousers
the moon hangs over us its grey flag
plays over us its unkind light.

Should

The pelt of the entity should be collected and left on the stretchers. Its skin should be cased pelt-side-out. The armature shaft should be turned until the number 1 appears at the peephole. The upper end of the body-wire should be cut. The test light should light in the LOCK position and go out in UNLOCK. The pawls should be depressed, and should be rendered by the argon washout technique. R&D projects should be turned over to the private sector. The sailing directions for Bass Harbor should be followed. Duck Rocks tripod should be seen northward, vessels should pass north of the whistling buoy. The sandpaper should be folded over a piece of wood so as not to spoil the shear studs. The input LED indicator should be used to check this. The parties seeking relief should turn to the north during the day, and to the south during the night. Their biceps should finish in line with your ears. Should the switch fail to turn off after a pulse operation the contactor should be used as a safety device. The indicator should remain on as the forks lower and turn off when the forks are level. The cache should result in uniform execution time. System shut-down applications should pull data from the server. High velocity hoods should be located late in the dryer section. A botanist should accompany the contract administrator periodically. Frequency shifter engines should take up the suite of values embodied in the trailing shock. The fruit-bearing shoots should produce more cock-to-cock conflicts, occasionally screams. You should explain to your team where the shoal is going or how it should behave. When the Weather-god comes to heaven, he should not approach the king. He should be covered with a veil lest his breath should offend. The solid red ball should fit the tube closely. Execution of the fake should be sharp and crisp. Paths should be seen as defective in that they lack inherent endpoints. A void field should be disallowed: this method of examination should not be used. The spindle should be raised or lowered by means of the spindle nut, the hold-down clamps should be bowed slightly. The aim should always be to finish the job in one heat. The policy community should receive the events data, then the PicoDrive menu should appear on your screen: compression of the sheath distal to the injection site should be applied. The compliance office should not be located within the offices of other corporate executives. The clock should be made independent of time. A system of corrugated-board standards should encourage cost reduction and optimum allocation of resources should take account of the requirements of different categories of box contents and should be based on test methods. If the packing is adequate the carrier should regard it as a burn hazard. His eyes should be bandaged, and the magnetiser taken from the blister-pack. It should fit snugly; integrity should be verified using a hash function. Poetry should hurt, should be part of this world. Turquoise stones inside the hole feel dryer than they should. This room should be used for worshipping of the rice goddess. Functionality should be built-in. Sleep should be irrelevant, unnecessary, and unsatisfying. The past will not be resisted but should. You shoulder the present, push it past the inner monuments.

Richard Berengarten

from The Wine Cup
Drinking Songs for Tao Yuanming

Dark Blaze

How many of us find the way of ways
that has no name? There's one reply: Who knows?
I sip my wine and relish its dark blaze.

I pour another cup. How the light plays,
changing across the sky in streaks and glows!
How many of us find the way of ways?

Tracking the rising moon through summer haze
after my work is done, as the light goes,
I sip my wine and relish its dark blaze.

Dissolve desire? Stop searching? Simply praise?
Another cup, perhaps, before repose?
How many of us find the way of ways?

See fireflies flicker in their damp arrays
down by the brook. Longing for dreamtime grows.
I sip my wine and relish its dark blaze.

Dusk thickens and my eyesight ebbs and sways.
Forgetting is a way too, I suppose.
How many of us find the way of ways?
I sip my wine and relish its dark blaze.

Empty house

I drink alone, half-sleeping, half-awake,
billowed by half-thoughts I can hardly bear.
Old friend, I'm just a ripple in your wake.

Just yesterday I rowed across the lake
to have a drink with you. Now in despair
I drink alone, half-sleeping, half-awake.

It's spring again. Ice melts. Flood waters break.
I'd packed a jar of wine for us to share.
Old friend, I'm just a ripple in your wake.

A plump bird flitted past. A coot or crake?
I knocked. Nobody opened. You weren't there.
I drink alone, half-sleeping, half-awake.

Was that house yours? My dream? Or my mistake?
Dust filled the place. Its cobwebbed cupboards bare.
Old friend, I'm just a ripple in your wake.

You've vanished like the dawn into daybreak
and hardly left a shadow anywhere.
I drink alone, half-sleeping, half-awake.
Old friend, I'm just a ripple in your wake.

Chrysanthemums

Whatever is, has form. What's born becomes
death-fruit – death being birth's corollary.
Autumn is back with gold chrysanthemums.

Everything's ripened – apples, damsons, plums,
I've picked them, twisting each stem carefully.
Whatever is, has form. What's born becomes.

I've rubbed skin-bloom off fingers, licked my thumbs,
sucked juices out. Such sensuality!
Autumn is back with gold chrysanthemums.

I'm still in rapture. Consciousness succumbs
to this abundant prodigality.
Whatever is, has form. What's born becomes.

I still hear bee-hordes. My whole being thrums.
I pick flower-heads to dry for wine and tea.
Autumn is back with gold chrysanthemums.

Blackbirds peck berries. Sparrows, fallen crumbs.
And me? Drunk without drinking, on a spree.
Whatever is, has form. What's born, becomes.
Autumn is back with gold chrysanthemums.

Mark Goodwin

A Glen Arnisdale & A Gleann Dubh Lochain, A Spring Start 2018

as spring's f orms jell
and sun's old

est of new

gest

ures un
furls

here

as

                    is

       .

Glen Arn
isdale holds

its burn's gli
de in a

fold

made of

past
ure wo

ods &

hills
ide a

fold seam
ingly solid

as an   alm
an

ac's

time see   ms
to be not

ched in
mind

a so
ng of

some bird not

thru   sh but
like holds

all this

fold's solids
now

in a fluid

                                    of s
                ad's

                            gl

ee

                    .

at *Gleandubhlochain* (as

OS have it at a

round NG 908103)

where a power

line held
up by lit

tle pylons re
lays

the punch
of electrons

one

                    mature rowan grows
                    ever older in a

ruin of

cottage peopled
by corp

ulent gleaming green

ferns

Simon Smith

Angel Road

I look upon you with utter delight
that's my job

operating well in excess of recommended safety levels

halo/hallo/hallelujah
my life of distractions

caught on the entry camera
is to have no memory is to have
no enemy

this is a Love poem
in the poem's embrace that loves the World
like a new (invisible) planet

beyond
unnamed cosmic dust
there all the days of humankind

& more
in my life of distractions

in series
in this envelope between
earth & stratosphere

twelve miles high
crash out stay put
therefore this poem doesn't exist

the place of removal
thinking things out
thinking things through

thinking things
I don't know why when
it all feels wrong

there's no moving forward
& how I miss you & howl
symptoms synapses

& signposts through the eyes
buds to statistical analyses

conduct oneself with grace is the goal
as a line of poetry

a flower on the mouth

Poem After the End of Time

its when I see a shape it comes
marks its arrival
& the politics are your call

while the destruction of the World grinds away

she had the aura that broke me
& if I can't have you then I'll fill the page

because
Time no longer exists
History no longer exists

Politics no longer exists
extending into the endless future
heat wave floating in off the ocean

& that's the Law
we all lay down in

in the present climate everything takes on a new shade

pours out & scrap all 'Culture'
I mean pressing hard
pressing forward

as images twist in the air

past the tipping point crowd into mob
the demagogue knows his Lenin
& the politics have eaten my tongue

as a naked man drinking coffee
I am swallowed by a bed

the maid singing in the next room
sweet & truly anonymous

all to herself
in all its political agency

it is the time to step
back a step
turn out of my depth

beats hard upon the tongue
when its best to keep an eye

on all the colours
of all the hundreds & thousands

when all the poem can do is wriggle
listen outside the musical pattern

with it

speak Truth to sing
my heart in ashes
alive between everything

what I'm saving all my human teeth for
from my particular little corner of the World Wide Web
when I've spent the day in orange socks

its as though to step through the mirror
to the side of the Dead

when fill a page will not do
the trees form a kind of lettering

an area an aura an era
lost sight of

when the debris floats by the window
then there's the call to signs

Susie Campbell

A Deictic Miracle, this Boxwood Prayer Nut

(Waddesdon Bequest, 1510)

'I made them contained within the thing I wrote that was them. The thing in itself folding itself up inside itself like you might fold a thing up to be another thing which is that thing' —Gertrude Stein

To hold and be held, an uncracked walnut, a little earth. There is something strange about this richness, growing into its own boundaries, rank and subtle as a hunted creature. Time has become a strongbox of interlocking branches. Global complexities, plumbed with pipelines of gold, are reduced to wafer-thin discs, slotted one into the other, light bevelled into a compound syntax of mortise and tenon. An articulation of honest wood, it holds the shape and hard veins of the forest by fitting it to the palm: an armillary sphere circling an internal sun, opened by flicking up a tiny hinge secured on its pin. Ahead, glimmering through a tiny screen, carved and fretted to this terrestrial cage, a thimble saint with his trembling hound bows before the stag. Kneeling here, prayer beads in hand, an intricate system of shadow blows from antler and slender branch to form the cross, thorn-sized and lifted to the wooden sky, as outside bends to imitate this reconciliation.

Arriving

We use the present perfect tense to talk about things where there is a connection between the past and the present. The present perfect continuous suggests something is unfinished. (*Learn English*, British Council)

Standing out here while the present slants back to an unstable sun, we have been crumbling, waiting. No vantage, paper-thin, if there isn't any origin or arrival which moors us to a red- and blue-striped post, but as the moon swings up over this busy port we have something that started then and continues on the rise and fall.

These have been travelling days; our shadow has been giving ground to doubt. That unnamed young woman, whose front teeth were knocked out by the butt of a rifle, cannot be the same young woman who has been waiting in the doorway of our house.

This belief in our continuation while we have been standing here, in its arrival sails straight past us, slewing away from the present towards a red horizon.

Elżbieta Wójcik-Leese

tropospheric turn in Douglas Fir's overstory

in this high blue clearing
I'm one with the clouds

like them I've left the Dalradian
rocks and etymology
insistent on facing down

I've learnt to counteract
by assuming the upside

my upper branches of pliant
green join now the white cumuli
in their feathery glide north

my soft flat needles upturn
their undersides to align
each pair of whitish stripes
with the drift lines
of water vapour
and crystal ice

I too move

over the Birnam Slates
and Dunkeld Grits

over the furrowed fields
moor heather grass

over the shimmer
of lochs
and lochans

towards the Highland Boundary Fault

and beyond

no longer rooted
in earth

rooted
for as long as it lasts
in this wind

Notes:
* 'troposphere,' the name for the lowest region of the atmosphere, derives from the Greek 'tropos,' i.e. 'turn, turn toward, change'; 'cloud' comes from the Old English 'clud/clod,' that is, 'rock/hill' and was applied to 'cumulus' at the end of the 13th century; 'overstory' is the specialist term for forest canopy.

** 'The structures in the Dalradian rocks near the Highland Border of Scotland consistently face downwards. They are upside-down.' Robert Millner Shackleton, 'Downward-facing structures of the Highland Border,' *Quarterly Journal of the Geological Society* 113 (1 Oct 1957) 361.

second take

now she feeds the shadow
    of the tree that stood here
        vast and luminous
            digesting light
                so enviously
                    guarded in the north

across its absence she discerns
        the other trees so far
           overshadowed
             not acacias
                spruces their branches
                    burdened with the wind
                        well past midnight

behind the double glaze
    of the dark she swallows the white
        capsule with aspirin
           waits for it to release the sap
                of the trunk
                cut

Andrea Moorhead

Lying away from the darkness

as if night were a function of the body
a turning over of neurons
in obscure sections of the brain
influenced by solar waves
skin stretching out of shape
the tongue dangling droplets of light
speech so far away
the other end of the cortex
the sudden lacuna perceived
as the eyes gaze farther and farther away

Rejection

Huddling under the fires, it's all in your mind, the burning trees, the molten ground, the heaviness of smoke in your lungs, huddling under the snow, it's not true, the searing cold, the crackling snap of trees, the pungent clarity of the sky, huddling under the barren wind that brings in nothing, the blackened rivers of your blood revolt, and these words tear a furrow through speech, eradicate the need for conversation, anything that escapes your lips will be condemned as the ravings of a semi-conscious maddened being, stranded in a snow bank or half buried under the blazing ground.

If the Earth

A pattern of sutures
catches the light
your skin still bleeding
autumn leaves wet gravel
the sound of another wind returning
debris from other worlds, other times
your eyes are shot with silver
weeping the rain slowly
each crystalline reflection snags
my eyelashes
blue powder on the hairs
there is no capillary action here
snow as a compression
to check stray migration
or the trembling of another heart
too close to feel.

If we could become dreams

rising and falling from the tight line between clouds, from the mast of a
phantom boat, lost in wrinkles and creases when the shore lights are too
strong, bending over as the water rises, piled so high on a child's drawing
that the tops of the waves are crystalline, emitting shrill notes every time
we plunge into the night, pulling octopus and squid from their sheltering
depths, and the rocks roll over us and the stars find another orbit, far to
the south on a dusty night, marked by iron bands deep beneath the molten
crust, you can't tell how many chimes should ring nor what the form of the
ice will be, alphabets are written in the wrinkles creases folds, when we lie
awake at night on a phantom ship, watching the world slip away.

Sarah Watkinson

Rural Assets, Blenheim

Underfoot's not dirt, not soil – but earth,
skin of the planet where we live, allowed by leaves.
This morning bluebell shoots poke up. It's spring!
Moss glows green in the wood, paths run with water,
snails are on the move. Sun spotlights the palace.
Let's deny our dread at the jaundiced field,

think instead how like prairie a huge field
can feel; how a sea of barley covered the earth
last summer, foreground to a vista of the palace.
Let's pretend we're not offended at the dead leaves
of sprayed-off oat grass, forget our fear that water
flows nitrate-glutted even from the spring.

The farmer's doing his best. We spring
to his defence and praise how the field
is spread with sewage sludge, how flood water
drains off through new ditches, how gaily his earth-
moving JCB shines through quickthorn bare of leaves,
his entangled banks richer than the lawns of the palace.

The park is let for shooting; corporations fill the palace
with away-days and silver service lunches; by late spring
guides will talk of Blindheim, seen through tapestry leaves
on the eve of battle; show private rooms; *Tatler, The Field*
on rosewood tables; the animatronic ghost. Who on earth
eats round a rococo gold centrepiece? The ground water

that rises at Rosamund's Well – unholy water –
sells for souvenirs, custom-bottled for the palace,
linked to a legend: King Henry and his girl, the earth
briefly theirs alone, the wildwood leaf-dark in spring

myth-haunted, concealing, with no house or field
near; horned figures, magic, eyes behind the leaves.

Then, only autumn yellowed the leaves,
lakes and streams glittered with living water.
The ploughman dreamed his fair field
full of folk who'd never see a palace –
new grass and milk made their spring,
creatures beyond imagining, their earth.

This spring walking leaves earth on my boots. My house is no palace
but I have hot water; and my study, where I write and field calls.

Corporate Q and A

'What does it take to be a truly effective board?'
    I am proud of my straight grain, strength and resilience. Ten of us
were delivered by a Stenner saw, from a felled oak dragged in chains from
a southern wood.

'Discuss the importance of clearly defined roles,'
    I will always feel vertical at heart, though now I am alone and
horizontal. The wind no longer stretches me, I have no roots to resist it.
    I am dried and abraded, waxed and polished smooth. My legs have
made me immobile. The Board members admire my fine figuring:
heartwood and sapwood, knots from branches lost to deer in my green
days, even the tawny spalting from a rot that my young tissues resisted.
    Spring is for their AGM, not my rush of sap. In the wood I bore acorns
and suffered squirrels, now I am papered over with their accounting.

'and setting achievable goals'
    In the beginning they made us for gift, communion and sacrifice. A
board can host a faculty, give or withhold approval; aspire to sanctity as
altar, or gravitas in its board-room.

'in our latest corporate governance article.'
    I may be board now, but know this: only weather and daylength
governed the wood where I grew.

David Sergeant

from Common Sonnets

My identity I think is worry
And a visionary glimpse of a monopoly
Scarcely acknowledged, on these clouds, even as it slips
Into the terroir of History, an exemption from which
Was its power, the exemption from identity
Its gift, notwithstanding the boutique pass
It handed out to aisles of dates and nouns
And powdered wigs. Counting back you reach 8,
A rhyming word, to heave and hoick
Into the plot the cliff in the sailor's storm
That feels like a bedrock and would make
For an easy fate, the orgasmic
Annihilating embrace of Master and Slave.
You have said the words, and set that hare running.

*

Hard not to be a preacher when sat
In the passenger seat and the last zebra
On earth has wandered out from its crossing
In dream-conspiracy with tortured cows
Straight into your road, hard not to yell
And feel your bladder ding ding on your heart
Like a supposedly neutral umpire on a boxer's bell –
But O, my friend, myself, when you wake and see
You're the driver, I'm curious
And genuine, what do you yell out then?
Take it as a symptom I'm sometimes aware of
That your presence still seems available
Without question and corresponding
Behind my back with the letters on the page.

*

White, male, English middle class and heading
To middle age on a planetary heading
Of fuck-up. My hair goes blonde in sunshine
And it doesn't matter if you're starving.
I tan easily and that's dangerous.
On most statistical counts I'm lucky
But measuring what can't be measured
Might bring a different result for this place.
When I'm laughing I can't be measured
Or placed, when I'm crying I should be glad
I'm not starving, at least after, at least
Till we're ejected from this place. We should be kind
To one another, said Philip Larkin, not a nice man.
But he felt it then, I'll give him that, it's worth nothing.

*

I mean the opposite of hate, said Bloom, very nearly,
And I'm remembering as well the popular song
You're thinking of now that's everywhere.
We exist in the same space, though the money's different.
The least you can do is not vote
For your second home and kill everybody
Over the age of fifty. I'm joking
At least half of the time. I'm snarky
And have a point, whatever the haters say.
The least you can do is not have a family
Unless it consists of at least a hundred people
Loosed from blood and running on the sun.
I'd wish that on my beautiful son,
An economy of scriptless love.

*

Nadira Wallace

Surrender Harder!

0. [Ars Poetica

I like a long tongue which can reenter the past,
and get to licking there with phrases;
get to massaging there
my injured ago's.]

1. First Love

We woke up and the deeper dream we had been dreaming clung to us
    groggily.
We woke up and saw the lawns of April framed by extending and nonsense
    space.
We woke up and found we had erections where there had previously been
    simple air.
Mine was chilly like Orion's spear. I felt it swaying above the earth, her
    scuffed Adidas,
broken membranes of plastic arranged like cards for solitaire.

I am still awake,
but tap these computer keys using fingers that're stiff: ten freckled caskets.
There needs to be another awakening
before I can properly lie down,
                and with you rest.

2. Apology

10+ swigs of bourbon, not bourbon really, but a fount of

1. ballistic vests,
2. whistles for summoning the super-black compassion of a night,
3. cotton-wool for winding around 200 million cars
    that were coughing lustily
    a dirt-cumulus,
    earlier.

On Western Avenue and 24th Place,
I was worrying about my weakness but now I'm fine, really,
drunk as a hit-skunk,
leathery paws to the sky—

while I am taking in the unexcavated shadows around your human belly
and inside its button, as you bend down
and come close,
proving it's possible to be close again,
and also that we, who have held to childhood's flame-gun of promise,
aren't such fools.

3. Hangover
This sunset is inundating my eyes, ouch, the whole colour-spectrum of regret.
There's vomit in a large Nike-swoosh down the side of our 4-Runner.
And the warehouses opposite haven't budged, squat and white, like molars…

Unintoxicated time,
she takes the throne again
and wags a finger at me:
remember the seed from which you sprang,
you were not made to drive your blossomy
attention back underground,
but to branch into this rain-slashed charity.

4. 2013—
was the year my original name flew off like a bird
to find a more secure perch.
That one outing, we could have had these labels pinned to us, though:
lesbian-loser/stockholder + sex-worker,
wrapped in the sun's hair streaming to unending radius.

I said: *I'll un-break you with plenty of twenties*—
later at the hotel (it was a *Hilton* with pig-
obstinate windows). That's when the MDMA-high started to melt
and run down the wall-paper,
like tear-tassels—without impairing, however, the vision I had brought
            with me

to our rendezvous: your ex-paralegal hands closing
around my grey-steak heart, before kneading
it back to quickness. Next day,
while driving south beneath Indiana's trembling powerlines,
I got a text: *well, boredom hasn't killed me yet!*

5. Nowhere to Hide
Human mixing has left a sore.
And it isn't terribly useful anymore:
this laying my head in your lap in order to blank out outside
(for instance, the spellbound hair
of cuboid bushes). I heard Mohammed tried to do that,
as he was being stalked on every side
by an angel with a sword in its grip, unsparing as noon-sun.

6. Extra
When I look up I feel I'm home-come—
why? What have those shreds of dream-fleece, clouds, got to do with me?

Perhaps I'm more than slow-capsizing skin?
Perhaps there's something, sky-allied, that would like to levitate this
        mammal frame?

7. My Soul at 24
was like a black passionfruit; most of the time, aspiring to leave my body
        &—*wham*—
crack every watch-face on earth.
Because the point was to go home to the wordless sanity
of building Lego castles before school—
when I knew
I was everyone instinctively,
and that I could tuck the Milky Way
under one of my earlobes,
if asked.

8. Risky Business
One day at a time, all I've got to worry about is taking after the three Pierides.
Those girls who presumed to match the Muses
with their bratty art. And who became like magpies, as a result—

squawkers and hoppers after tinsel bits.

All I've got to worry about is not being able
to see me. Those girls. Till they died, a cranial mud
sat behind nine pairs of eyes. What was left, then? Not works, just warning.

9. *The Rope of Faith*
Made out of bee wings and flower pistils glued together, using a newborn's
spit bubbles, the rope of faith doesn't have a visible end—but it promises to
take us up levels, past mezzanines of frown, quizzical eyes dashing stucco—
higher and higher, till we start to reach balconies of real adroitness. No
more fear-blanched brain then, baby, nor that shivering that defrauds us of
day-pearl after day-pearl!

10. *Spring*
Warbles Demeter, goddess of cereal grains: *my daughter's resurfaced
from under rubber treads. She's tricked the king of death and skips now—
up and down, catalyzing hedgerows, handing out green leaflets on survival.*

*You there, still hampered, still chthonic, still handcuffed, look this way and
be encouraged! My arms, which were thin switches for dragging months,
have become petaloid again …   look this way, this is Spring!*

11. *'Good Old Days'*
When it felt like we were precious, sharing a level—
receiving equal quotas of clement sunbeam … no one
promoted yet, no one pan-handling by office-block's vent
with a torn nose-ridge yet … before failing's floor-less-ness.
The body: magazine-clip-like, holding supplies and supplies for
firing into the future; no one mutinied mentally yet or mud-paneled.

12. *Resurrect*
Looking at a daffodil's saw-toothed silk—
my head feels held, my head that used to be pretty darn lust-concussed.

What Winter monotonized is greening up and out.

Some repairer present, I reckon. Some repairer who is
stashing in each cell—doesn't matter how cold or craven—evermore
        sunbreaks.

Alexandria Peary

Sonnet branches

The forearm of spring rests on the window sill
to the kitchen where I'm boiling opera for pasta.

This branch of spring is a real interloper,
a man's arm covered in hard yellow blossoms,
No. 2 yellow, like a line of forsythia
in inter-winter-spring. Other sonnet branches
are scattered in the backyard, fourteen limbs
decked out in the *darling buds of May*.
The man's branch intrudes through the open
window in early spring, so it's a line in a poem.

Those italicized and underlined branches
about timeless beauty, a love w/out physical detail,
maybe the pivot toward writing and the writer,
I'll have to pick up after them after dinner,

I'll organize w/ a ladybug red wheelbarrow,
kindling for prose or a Triskelion.

Social Media Ensō

Look daily, check every
                20 minutes inside this gate
                                of calligraphy made
                                                with a single brushstroke
mirror mirror on the wall
                a background of vowels
                                o—ohm like eyeholes
                                                split screen   ego is lessness
a white scroll for Facebook
                who's the smartest status
                                update *sexiest wealthiest*
                                                busiest talented of them all
Notice a pattern of skulls
                in the social stationary
                                Dead Heads or deadhead
                                                a long haul without paying
passengers or freight or
                to ride without buying a ticket
                                dead flowers snapped away
                                                to encourage others to bloom
with encrypted information
                because you lost your i-
                                phone, pod, pad
                                                in an underground tomb
& 100,000 early Christian martyrs
                like adults at a sleepover
                                see the screen illuminate
                                                in the ashen dark
as you send yourself a message
                where are you
                                & try to summon your lost be-
                                                longing from the hotel room
this is no ordinary love
                a brushstroke to represent the moment
zeitgeist.

Hannah Star Rogers

Good news, I have been advised, you live in your head

I mourn you like the wind
over a hollow cave our

hollow cave where I can go
but can never be

the hallowed world howls
the animal fur mind taints

any recollection save the
bequest of the the body

the passenger rocks
make possible the irony

of sand. the volatility of time,
lurching behind another place.

Chicken Ain't Nothing But a Bird

The work
He did was
Making animals.

All that is real are
My memories of
Saying chicken, bird.

Eggplant stems,
Touch-me-nots, mimosas
Dried, become feed, scratch

Shells of mussels,
Limestone slivers from the ossuary
Mineralize new eggs, dog food.

The morning gloat
Of what was once only holy
Denies wholeness.

Peter heard the birds
Their portraits only tronies,
Ledgers in the barn.

The work
Animals do is
Animal work.

Apricot Forms

Open to the impression of the stars
Unwilling in their glory to stop for time

Our mouths shut to the possibility
Of their blaze and signing out

The movement as like us, as like
The life wanting to be recognized

As unfolding or at least a little change
Blessed by motion we long for permanence

The opposite of the triangle of
Place and position makes waves

I cannot gather in the fabric, cannot
Reconcile to loss, will shine instead.

Denni Turp

grounded

leaning over
      head down in submission
            back bent like a Capuchin
            monk in silent prayer
but with antennae poised
as if seeking some response
some sign from the still cold air
                    you are
      nonetheless so beautiful
             in death

small
glistening
dual wings
                up
as if alert for flight
       & caught like that
legs splayed
supportive
yet
      without messaging to come
you leave your shadow
on the wall
       like a tiny hand
             at play

The Grim Reaper

might come with all guns blazing,
Stetson tipped and gun belt slung
low around his hips, legs wide,
feet planted hard, and half a smile
before he bends to kiss your lips;
might lure you with performance,
a velvet-costumed swagger and
a lovely turn of phrase that forces
your applause; might merely be
the steady drip of liquid, a need
for change, repair, retrenchment;
might paint it violet, the indigo
of night, wafting lavender and tossing
sand to make you rub your eyes;
or might just shout a sudden Boo
to shock you off from where
you had believed you would be safe
before you realise.

Sunburnt

Diving off the barges on the River Lea,
he went swimming as a lad, dried off in the sun,
fell asleep aboard the resting, quiet decks.
Red-haired and freckled, more than once
that napping was a bad mistake that cost him pain
and later even shame, resulting in a sudden faint
while stood in line with other brave cadets at school,
where he was thrown out, labelled as unfit
for army service training even though a child.
Close on eighty years ago, and he can
laugh it off now, make it just a story,
just a joke, though the details linger
undeniably: ginger boy falls asleep on boat.

Kit Hanafin

Farm Drama 2020: White House Murders

To get to the ending you already
know, you must go around the
houses, past the brick building set
in England's mastered prairie, her
silent wheat fields apt to seethe
     at a breath of mercy, here
are the murders unfolding again on
television, pity declines to
the mirrored family cloistered
in the inner chamber of a
sponsored grain economy/ was
heat the mystery that eluded
us?/ the victims retired indoors from
the light of August, it is the same

blank light of high definition,
falling on gleaming sheaves,
the twins warming in their beds
like wuffled hay prepared for
threshing on the homestead floor,
a rakish villain stepping through
his likeness in the aftermath
and vomiting, they say, a comb
is present and correct in a hair
brush, blood has dried like paint
on the floor, the inspector is
a buffoon, with his unsteady
footwork, scuffing the gravel
driveway to the charnel

my heart is aching for
that poor man, one viewer wrote,
who's lost his baby boys (Don't
miss Love Island 2020, winner already
revealed thanks to famous ties?)
I could slip inside with the police,
blind to one another cruelty
and curiosity could follow me,
                rejoice
                & fumble stick in
hand triumphant to disaster/
kindness tramples the soft toys
and blunders in the golden stubble
                    hiding its eyes

Conversation

Uncertain as we walk if it's towards
the light, away from that obsidian curve
behind us, a cliff of opaque glass,
answer me as a reader talks to
a poem, whose train of thought
is grounded in specific love of
landscape, figured in local diction,
grist to a sense of commonwealth
or merely a model of how
we'd converse beyond the page, as
listeners so to speak – & you deserve
a hearing   one day we hope,
your sweet free-ranging verse
will overrun the citadel by stealth

Luke Palmer

In all my books my father dies

-i-

Seated in a throne-like chair — Father.

A magnificent suite of rooms, a garden
   smell of lemon trees
               Inside
sofas deep as small ships.

Arms held out   massively leonine.
                Eyes
     two slabs of mahogany
             Mouth
     surprisingly delicate.

Imperial he was.   All huge.   Enormous.

He decided very quickly, lowered his soul
to unconscious form
            blood
leaking through his body

               Terrible times

merciful deeds.

He   grievously wounded   held
on the other side of the fence
            among the undying.

-ii-

Like a queen by the small lake
                         (my father already dying
                         not like people can't see it)
every night my mother a coppery mass.
                                        My
mother-on-the-floor
never complained   thought it impossible.

Before God she repeated little platitudes
                                  that
    if he'd wanted to he could have –
                                  and
    he was the one who loved her best.

She'd say of his death
                    what an awful thing.
Our little kinship
   remains
at the dining room table.

          -iii-

My father thought he could hide in my stomach
a great big knot that lied   worms
and maggots.

His voice started to hammer
against the walls
                loud clunks in the cradle.

Father full of tears
— whole head ready to burst   breath
between heaves   vomit-coughing —

ease the ache in my stomach.
                              By god
what a state to get yourself in

I know my shivering. The chills
tell me I died at just the right time, yielding

to a smooth black future. I am
no longer among the quick but I have memory left.

I try to list my children.
I've got ghosts and children from ear to ear.

The first few swell to greet me;
a rousing tribute.

I am disposed to glow. Beguiling father
on my deathbed neither here nor there.

Don't worry
don't worry.

Bathe him
                Let him shiver
if he doesn't want to go.

The poems in this sequence are sculpted from books published in 1984. The same page
numbers are used from each book and the words appear here in their original order.
The texts used are as follows:

i – *The Sicilian* – Mario Puzo
ii – *The Lover* – Marguerite Duras
iii – *The Wasp Factory* – Iain Banks
iv – *God Knows* – Joseph Heller

Paul Rossiter

North

the train halts

windless silence, falling snow
visibility ten metres

twigs and branches, silver
birches muffled with heavy white

*

north-western coast
a sea in turmoil
among dark rocks

*

FUROUFUSHI ONSEN

a concrete path across a stony beach
        yukata flapping wildly in the gale
to an open-air hot spring exactly at
the sea's edge

        waves heave towards the land,
        sheets of foam criss-cross,
        overtake each other, subside
        into an agitation of blue water
        amongst black rocks beside the bath

steaming orange-brown
            mineral-laden water
a pink-orange sunset intermittently glimpsed
between grey roiling clouds

gulls swerve and dip
three rapid cormorants
       do a fly-by parallel to the shore

biting wind off the sea chills
the windward shoulder
fingers and toes
instantly numb on stepping from water into air

      furoufushi = 'no aging, no death'

*

the gale thumps, batters at
the flimsy building all night
loud enough to wake me, take me
to the window to watch

huge seas crashing to shore
waves tripping over
themselves and tumbling headlong
in a seethe of white

in the grey dawn
a hailstorm rattles the breakfast room windows

*

MORNING BUS

coastal villages
potholes and empty houses
no one to be seen

*

wind strong enough to have rolled newly fallen snow
into snowballs, to have trundled these across the
freezing white plain – leaving a tangled
skein of tracks behind them – until,
too heavy to be shifted further,
they came to rest, stranded
here and there in their
random not-random
places

*

AOMORI

apples and grown-under-snow carrots
fish from northern ports

in the hush after
the shinkansen's departure
boot soles creak on snow

Charles Wilkinson

le vent

a late hour wind sawing into sleep.
through a window a curl of moon
caught between clouds; length of a howl
powered down & deep, shrilling into
the mountain pass; rain-rap right-angled
to the wall, one drip as if starlit, glint-flow
on glass…
          so stunned back to the dream
& high bare hills polished to an inch
of grass … awake again to the stars
    strewn wild across
       the carpenter's floor.

     from slumber to cold morning
& wind-swagger still caught lumbering
about the trees; to the west the blast
quickens into the gap: so a sting in light,
charged & white, its movement alive,
as if chemical

       far above level ground,
grey black rain-fleece, dishevelling
in the gales, slides on the glacial face
of higher cloud stacked square
to the troposphere, soundless beyond
the crack of ice & without motion,
as if spellbound, pinned to the top
of eternity, outside the spin of earth,
its racing storms –
         the quietest place,
lacking haste: wordless white paradise.

courant

running as a way the world stretches breath, white tail of a comet
  converting to cloud, the dissolve behind you, cross-country slant
  of the mud fields beneath the shoes, the blue sky set to the moment
  of spin, the sweat that seals skin from the wind, the tug of the track
downhill, one foot on the style then over, speed fixed to leap the stream,
  angle of shadow seen for a second on water-flow; climbing
to the crest as a form of war, the rope path pulling you back, then
  across the flat of the meadow, their voices distant but cheering,
the taut line holds the finish taped, till even the winner's bent
  to a double, his shadow swaying towards a crucifixion.
& so hard to think of a running saviour, he who walked, even
  when on water, steadying the waves beneath footfall. think of
the river in riot, its white flash leaving a half moon of air
  under the bridge, the torrent's many voices ripped over stone
roar, so again the clouds pillowing, amassed over the far black
  mountains, ready to blur, the first rain feathery in the mist,
waiting for the squeeze of isobars, then the thunder opens
  a door, the flood-wall breaks into bright veins & no redemption.
did the Buddha run? I think of his movements beneath the tree
  as minimal, less rapid than the circulation of divine blood.
now here are more runners: a gun sounding, the jostling colours
  & then the field narrowing to an arrowhead. above them,
where the sky's furious, all day the scud of clouds, not waiting
  for starter's orders. there's the leader, his arms & leg-flash flailing
over turf, as if to outpace his inconstant shadow, & his mouth
  is open, his spit will return on the wind to streak his hot cheeks.
he begs for the end of the race, for one still moment on earth.

Sylvie Marie

translated by Richard Berengarten & the author

Awkward

think of me as a scrap of paper
you absent-mindedly stuff in your pocket
after writing something on it. no matter what

though I hope: let it be a line, one for some
future stanza which keeps on coming
back to you long after you've tucked me away.

sooner or later you'll know the line inside out. it'll pop
up in your mind like a mantra. still, you can never
quite find where to fit it; a good poem
that places the line, frames it, yes, tames it.

so by then, you'll fish me out again,
stroke me and sigh, 'what am I going to do with you?'

Find Me

Poetry turns paper back into trees
—Marie Lundquist

find me   i'm standing
among the others   feet planted
in a corner   knees together
my woody trunk rising
through my resin pelvis

my backbone a
stem for starlings and fungus
my hips home to maggots and worms
my ribs branching for birds nesting

my bladed shoulders
bursting into leaf
spreading   high
as my lush canopy

and my arms   no   no
longer arms   i stretch   them
wide   out   around   me
sprigs   and   on every finger

a fresh fruit.

Notes on Contributors

KATE ASHTON lives in Nairn, on the Moray Firth. Her collection, *Who by Water*, was published by Shearsman in 2016. From 1979 until 2003 she lived, worked and wrote in the Netherlands, publishing full-length fiction and non-fiction. She has translated widely from Dutch and Flemish.

RICHARD BERENGARTEN has published a large number of books, many of which are available from Shearsman, such as *The Blue Butterfly* (2011) and *Changing* (2016). A collection of his essays and writings on the Balkans will be published by Shearsman in 2021.

GUY BIRCHARD lives on Vancouver Island, Canada, and has one book from Shearsman, *Aggregate: retrospective* (2018). Other recent publications include *Further than the Blood* (Pressed Wafer, Boston, 2010), *Hecatomb* (Pressed Wafer, Brooklyn, 2017) and *Only Seemly* (Pedlar Press, 2018).

DARAGH BREEN has two collections from Shearsman, most recently *Nostoc* in January 2020. He lives in County Cork, Ireland.

SUSIE CAMPBELL's most recent publication is *Tenter* (Guillemot Press, 2020). She is currently researching for a practice-based poetry PhD at Oxford Brookes University.

MAKYLA CURTIS is currently studying for a Masters of Visual Arts at Auckland University of Technology. Her work has previously appeared in a number of New Zealand publications (*IKA*, *Brief*, Blackmail Press, *REM Magazine*).

JODIE DALGLIESH is a writer, curator and sound artist living in Luxembourg. After over a decade of creating exhibitions for museums, she is now focused on poetry and fiction. She holds a Master of Creative Writing from AUT University, New Zealand.

GILES GOODLAND lives in West London, and is the author of a several books, two of them from Shearsman: *What the Things Sang* (2009) and *The Masses* (2018). Other recent publications have been *Gloss* (Knives Forks and Spoons, 2011) and *The Dumb Messengers* (Salt Publishing, 2012).

MARK GOODWIN has a number of books to his name, several of them from Shearsman, including *House At Out* (2015). Another, *At*, is currently in preparation.

LUCY HAMILTON co-edited *Long Poem Magazine* from 2008 to 2018, and now works for Cam Rivers Publishing. Her two collections of prose poems are *Stalker* (Shearsman, 2012), shortlisted for the Forward Prize for Best First Collection, and *Of Heads & Hearts* (Shearsman, 2018).

KIT HANAFIN, whose poems have been published in *Wretched Strangers* (Boiler House Press, 2018) and *PN Review*, is working on a long poem about the first Palestinian intifada and environmental degradation in Europe.

JILL JONES was born in Sydney and has lived in Adelaide since 2008. Her recent books are *A History of What I'll Become* (UWAP), *Viva the Real* (UQP) and *Brink*

(Five Islands Press). With Scots-Australian poet Alison Flett, she publishes chapbooks through Little Windows Press.

JOHN LEVY is an American poet based in Tucson, who has been involved with *Shearsman* magazine since its very beginnings in 1981.

JULIE MACLEAN is the author of *Tango Boleo* (with Avril Bradley, Ginninderra Press, Adelaide, 2019,) *Lips That Did* (Dancing Girl Press, Chicago, 2016), and *When I saw Jimi* (Indigo Dreams, 2013).

SYLVIE MARIE is a Flemish poet, from Ghent. Her first collection, *Zonder*, (Vrijdgag, Antwerp, 2009) was a great success in Belgium, and was followed by a novel and three more collections, the most recent being *Houdingen* (Vrijdgag, 2018). She is also an editor at the magazine *Deus ex machina*.

ANDREA MOORHEAD, editor of *Osiris* and translator of contemporary Francophone poetry, publishes in French and in English. Poetry collections include *The Carver's Dream* (Red Dragonfly Press), and *À l'ombre de ta voix* (Le Noroît). In 2018, she was awarded the Prix International de Poésie Antonio Viccaro.

DIANA MULHOLLAND was born in rural Australia and now lives in London. Her work has appeared widely in journals in the UK and Australia, including most recently *The Manchester Review, Finished Creatures, Not Very Quiet,* and *Long Poem Magazine*.

LUKE PALMER's debut pamphlet, *Spring in the Hospital* (Prole Books, 2018) was the winner of the Prole Pamphlet competition. His first novel is due for publication with Firefly Press in 2021.

ALEXANDRIA PEARY was recently appointed Poet Laureate of New Hampshire, and is the author of six books, including *Control Bird Alt Delete* (University of Iowa Press 2014) and *The Water Draft* (Spuyten Duyvil 2019).

JOHN PHILLIPS' most recent book, *Shape of Faith* (2017), is from Shearsman. His most recent publications are two chapbooks: *No Preference* (2018) and *Hourglass* (2020), both from Longhouse.

HANNAH STAR ROGERS' book-length collection of ekphrastic poems accompanied by the visual work that inspired them, *Exo-Sanctuaries*, is due out Fall 2020 from Bijou Art Books. Her first poetry monograph, *American Valentines*, will be published by Wesleyan University Press.

PAUL ROSSITER retired from teaching English and applied linguistics at the University of Tokyo in 2012 and in the following year founded Isobar Press. He has four books with Isobar, the most recent being *On Arrival* (2019) and three earlier volumes of his poetry have been published in Japan.

JAYA SAVIGE was born in Sydney and lives in London, where he lectures at the New College of the Humanities. His books include *Latecomers*, and *Surface to Air*, which was shortlisted for *The Age* Poetry Book of the Year. *Change Machine* is due from University of Queensland Press in late 2020.

DAVID SERGEANT is Associate Professor at the University of Plymouth, where he teaches modern literature. He has two collections to his name, *Talk Like Galileo* (Shearsman, 2010) and *The Pronoun Utopia* (Green Bottle Press, 2017).

SIMON SMITH has a *Selected Poems* (2016) with Shearsman, and a collection of translations from Catullus with Carcanet Press (2019).

SOPHIE (JIANGHONG) SONG, was born and grew up in China, and is now an editor for Cam Rivers Publishing. She lives in Cambridge with her husband and two children.

TUPA SNYDER lives in Calcutta. Shearsman published her first collection, *No Man's Land*, in 2007.

MARIA STASIAK grew up in Newfoundland and now lives in London. She has had work published in *Magma, The Rialto, Envoi, Iota, The North, Interpreter's House, Brittle Star, Urthona* and *Poetry Salzburg*.

JANET SUTHERLAND lives in Lewes, Sussex, and has four collections from Shearsman, the most recent of which is *Home Farm* (2019).

HELEN TOOKEY is based in Liverpool. She writes poems and short prose and has collaborated with musicians Sharron Kraus and Martin Heslop. She has published two poetry collections with Carcanet, *Missel-Child* (2014) and *City of Departures* (2019), and is currently working on a third.

DENNI TURP grew up in London but now lives in north Wales, where she graduated from Bangor University and pursued postgraduate research in Arthurian literature. Her poems have been published in a number of magazines, and she is a member of the Second Light Network of Women Poets.

NADIRA WALLACE is a practice-based PhD student at Royal Holloway, University of London. She received a BA and Masters from Oxford University before going on to study creative writing at the School of the Art Institute of Chicago.

SARAH WATKINSON is Professor emerita in Plant Sciences at the University of Oxford.

CHARLES WILKINSON's collection, *The Glazier's Choice*, appeared from Eyewear in 2019. He lives in Powys, Wales, where he is heavily outnumbered by members of the ovine community.

JUDITH WILLSON grew up in Manchester and lives in the Yorkshire Pennines. The poems in this issue will be included in her second collection, forthcoming from Carcanet in 2021, Her first, *Crossing the Mirror Line*, appeared from the same press in 2017.

ELŻBIETA WÓJCIK-LEESE writes with/in English, Polish and Danish. *Nothing More* (Arc, 2013), which samples the Polish poet Krystyna Miłobędzka, was shortlisted for the 2015 Popescu European Poetry Translation Prize.

Lightning Source UK Ltd.
Milton Keynes UK
UKHW010631200920
370211UK00001B/56